My Noah's Ark Book of COLORS

Books in this Series

My Adam and Eve Book of Opposites
My Noah's Ark Book of Colors
My Baby Jesus Book of Numbers
My Bible Story Book of ABC's

Copyright © 1995 by Educational Publishing Concepts, Inc., Wheaton, Illinois

Published by Concordia Publishing House
3558 S. Jefferson Avenue, St. Louis, MO 63118-3968
Manufactured in the United States of America

1 2 3 4 5 6 7 8 9 10   04 03 02 01 00 99 98 97 96 95

My Noah's Ark Book of COLORS

Glenda Palmer

Illustrated by
Rick Incrocci

CPH™
SAINT LOUIS

Why do we see a rainbow of colors after the rain?

Long ago, Noah and his family were the only people in the whole world who loved God.

God said, "Noah, it's going to rain. Build an ark. Build it with **brown** cypress wood."

Noah didn't say no. No way!

God told Noah how to build the ark.

Noah cut lots and lots of **brown** cypress wood.
Day after day, for a long time, Noah worked on the ark.
He built it just as God had said.

Then God said, "Noah, get two of every kind of animal and bring them into the ark."
Noah didn't say no. No way!

Noah opened the door and all kinds of animals paraded into the ark.

Big **yellow** lions and little **green** lizards.

Slippery **black** seals.
Furry **white** polar bears.
Black-and-**white** striped zebras.

Pink flamingos.
Orange orangutans.
Red-headed woodpeckers.
Big **gray** elephants and little **blue** birds.

All the animals marched into the ark, two by two.
Noah watched the long parade. God said, "Noah, you and
your family go into the ark."
Noah didn't say no. No way!

Noah and his family went into the ark, just as God said. God closed the door. The rain began *drip, drip, dripping;* *pitter, patter, pitter, pattering; rat-a-tat-tatting;* day after day, night after night, for forty days and forty nights.

Finally the rain stopped *rat-a-tat-tatting;*
and *pitter, patter, pitter, pattering;*
and *drip, drip, dripping.*
    Noah looked out the window and saw the **blue** sky!

Noah looked and looked at the **blue** sky. He wanted to go
out. But he waited for God to tell him when it was safe.
He waited . . .
     and waited . . .
          and waited.

At last God said, "Noah, now it is time to come out of the ark." Noah didn't say no. No way!

Noah and his family and the animals paraded out of the ark. Out came **brown** kangaroos and fluffy **white** rabbits. Tall **yellow** giraffes and smiley **green** crocodiles. Bright **red** birds and little **black** ants.

Noah and his family saw the shining **yellow** sun. They saw the bright **blue** sky. They stepped on soft **green** grass.

Noah said, "Thank You, God." He and his family and all the animals were safe.

Then God lit up the sky with the colors
of His rainbow—**red, orange, yellow, green,
blue, purple.**

God promised, "I will never again destroy the whole earth by water."

Noah was glad.
God never breaks a promise.
No way!